Deferred Action Guide For Virginia and DC Residents

WHAT EVERY VIRGINIA AND DC RESIDENT NEEDS TO KNOW BEFORE APPLYING FOR DEFERRED ACTION

Kimberley Schaefer
Attorney at Law

ImmigrationVirginia.com
(703) 424-2969

Deferred Action Guide For Virginia And DC Residents

What Every Virginia and DC Resident Needs To Know Before Applying for Deferred Action

by KIMBERLEY SCHAEFER

ISBN 978-0-9837391-6-6

Published by:
Maiesta Books
MaiestaBooks.com

Disclaimer

Deferred action for young immigrants is a new immigration policy. Because it is new, it is likely that the rules and requirements regarding the policy will change over time. In addition, this guide was initially written before any applications for deferred action were accepted. Once the government begins to accept applications and make decisions on individual cases, immigration lawyers will likely be able to provide you with additional guidance on your case.

The Publisher and the Author make no representation or warranties with respect to the accuracy or completeness of the contents of this work and specifically disclaim all warranties, including without limitation warranties of fitness for a particular purpose. No warranty may be created or extended by sales or promotional materials. Although every effort was made to ensure that the information contained herein was accurate at the time of publication, immigration law is constantly changing and the accuracy of the information contained herein may be affected by changes in immigration law. The information contained herein may not be suitable for every situation and is not legal advice specific to your situation.

If you need legal advice regarding your deferred action application or other immigration options, you should seek the services of an immigration lawyer. This book, even if received from Kimberley Schaefer or Schaefer Immigration, does not create an attorney client relationship between you and Schaefer

Immigration. Only a client representation agreement signed by both you and Kimberley Schaefer will create an attorney client relationship.

Books By Kimberley Schaefer

Adjustment of Status / Green Card Guide
for Virginia Residents
AdjustmentOfStatusBook.com

Do I Need an Immigration Lawyer?
ImmigrationLawyerBook.com

Family Immigration Guide
for Virginia Residents
FamilyImmigrationBook.com

Fiancé Visa Guide
for Virginia Residents
FianceVisaBook.com

Immigrant Visa Guide
for Virginia Residents
ImmigrantVisaBook.com

Immigration Mistakes You Can't Afford To Make
ImmigrationMistakesBook.com

Immigration Waiver Guide
for Virginia Residents
ImmigrationWaiverBook.com

Marriage Immigration Guide
for Virginia Residents
MarriageGreenCardBook.com

Introduction

Thank you for your interest in this deferred action guide.

This guide is for you if you are interested in learning more about the deferred action policy announced by President Obama on June 15, 2012. If you are reading this, you are probably trying to decide if you qualify for deferred action under this policy, whether you should apply for deferred action if you do qualify and how to apply.

This guide is intended to be a starting point and to help you better understand the new deferred action policy. Because the policy is new, there are many things that we don't know about the policy. The simple truth is that right now the only guarantee that anyone can give you about the policy is that you can't apply until at least August 15, 2012.

If you have decided to work with a lawyer to apply for deferred action, then you should read the section on finding the best immigration lawyer for your case before you hire a lawyer. As that section points out, your goal should be to find the best immigration lawyer for your case. Depending on your situation, I may not be the best lawyer for you. But my hope is that this book will help you get in contact with the best immigration lawyer for you.

If you have any questions about the deferred action policy and how you can work with me to better understand your immigration options and whether deferred action is right for you, please feel free to contact me at:

contact@ImmigrationVirginia.com

Office: (703) 424-2979
Toll free: (877) 887-9523

Schaefer Immigration
1818 Library Street, Suite 500
Reston, VA 20190

Table of Contents

Deferred Action Overview

Deferred Action

Deferred action is a temporary status that basically means that the government has decided not to move forward with deporting someone at the present time. The deferred action policy for childhood arrivals reflects the reality that the government has a limited budget and would like to prioritize its immigration enforcement activities to focus on criminals before they spend resources deporting people who are not criminals.

Some of the key things to keep in mind about deferred action for childhood arrivals:

- Deferred action is a temporary status. It does not give you any permanent right to remain in the United States. The government can still move forward with deporting you in the future.
- The government can terminate your deferred action status at any time.
- Deferred action is not an amnesty program. It does not forgive any past immigration violations.
- Deferred action does not provide a pathway to a green card.
- Deferred action does not provide a pathway to citizenship.

- There is no guarantee of how long you will be able to keep your deferred action status.
- The policy is subject to change at any time.

Qualifications for Deferred Action

Not everyone will qualify for deferred action. Some of the initial requirements that you should consider include:

- You must have entered the United States when you were under the age of sixteen.
- You must have continuously been in the United States since June 15, 2007 to the present time.
- You were physically present in the United States on June 15, 2012 and at the time you submit your application for deferred action.
- You must be in school, have graduated from high school, have a general education development certificate (GED), or be an honorably discharged veteran.
- You must not have ever been convicted of a felony offense, a "significant" misdemeanor offense, multiple misdemeanors, or be a threat to national security or public safety.
- You must have been under the age of 31 on June 15, 2012.
- Most applicants must be at least 15 years old.

The above list does not include everything that needs to be considered. If you work with an immigration lawyer, your lawyer will carefully review your situation to verify that you meet all of the requirements. If you don't meet the deferred action requirements, your immigration lawyer will be able to assist you in developing an immigration strategy that will help you find the best immigration option for you.

If you decide to apply for deferred action without the assistance of an immigration lawyer, you should carefully review all of the requirements before you submit any forms to the government. ***You should not rush to submit your forms.*** It will take time to learn the details of the deferred action process and to collect all of the required supporting documents, but this will be time well spent. After all, submitting your package if you don't meet all of the requirements or without the supporting evidence needed to win your case will result in significant delays and could possibly place you at risk of being deported.

Take the time to learn as much as possible about the deferred action process before you begin. If necessary, this includes doing legal research to understand the immigration consequences of any convictions that you may have (even expunged convictions, alternative sentencing programs and diversion programs). If you don't have the time or research resources to do this, you should try to work with an immigration lawyer.

Deferred Action Application Process

You can think of the deferred action application process in four steps:

Step 1: Review Requirements

The first step in applying for deferred action is to carefully review all of the qualifications listed in the last section. If you don't meet all of the qualifications, your application will be denied. If you aren't sure if you qualify, make sure that you discuss your case with a qualified immigration lawyer before doing anything else.

Step 2: Review Other Immigration Options

Reviewing your other immigration options isn't something that is officially part of the application process, but it is important that you take the time to think through your long term immigration options before you apply for deferred action. Deferred action is a temporary option that does not give you a way to become a permanent resident and get a green card. You should have a long term immigration strategy in mind before you submit your application.

In addition, you may have better options than deferred action. For example, you may be able to get a green card through the parole in place program if you are married to someone who is in the military. Some people who have been victims of crimes and who helped the police with their investigation may be eligible for U nonimmigrant status which can lead to a green card. Make sure that you understand all of your options before you decide whether deferred action is the right option for you.

Step 3: Collect Required Documents

The importance of this step can't be overstated. If you don't present the documents to prove that you qualify for deferred action, your application will not be approved. Don't be in a rush to submit your application and then end up not documenting your case well. A poorly documented application will likely result in a request for you to submit additional evidence. In other types of immigration applications, such as applications for a green card through adjustment of status, the applicant doesn't get their work card until after they respond to the request for additional evidence. This means that rushing your application could result in significant delays in getting your work card and in eventually being granted deferred action.

Step 4: Submit Application

After collecting all of the documents needed to prove that you qualify for deferred action and completing the application forms, you will then be ready to submit your application package. You should submit your package using a service that allows you to receive a delivery confirmation such as USPS delivery confirmation, FedEx or UPS. If possible, you may want to pay any application fees using a check to make it easier to verify that the government has received your fee and cashed your check.

Don't forget to keep a copy of everything that you submit to the government. This is especially true if you don't work with an immigration lawyer on your deferred action application. If you ever decide to work with an immigration lawyer at some point in the future, they will likely want to review your deferred action application during your initial consultation with them. In addition, having a copy of your deferred action application may make it significantly easier to reapply for deferred action when your initial deferred action expires in two years or to apply for other immigration options if they become available to you.

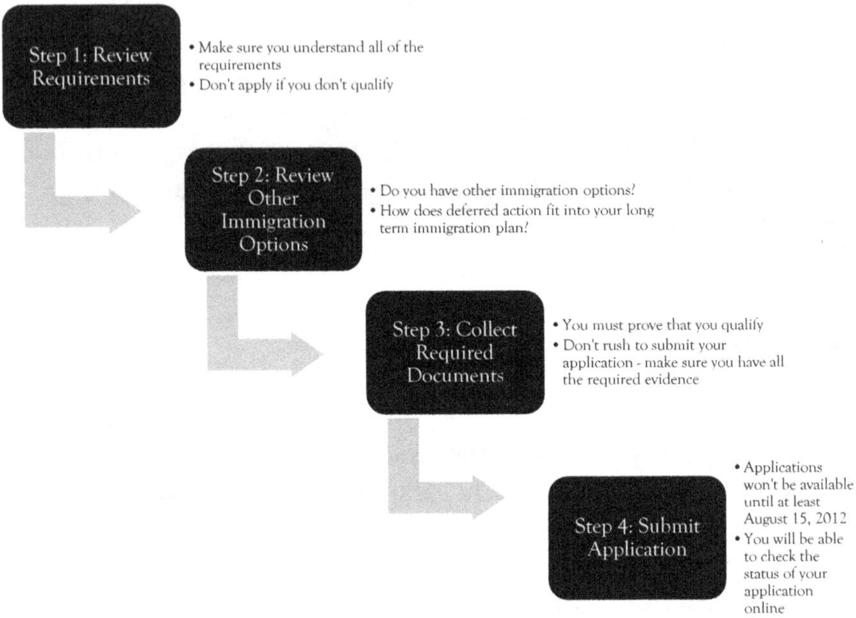

Figure 1 Deferred Action Application Process

Deferred Action Fees

The total cost for the entire process begins at $85 and goes up from there depending on whether you want to apply for a work card, need to pay for certified copies of documents or translations, or decide to work with an immigration lawyer.

Government Deferred Action Application Fees

$85 Required biometrics fee

$380 I-765 application fee for an employment authorization card (work card)

Other Required Costs

Passport photographs – changes by photographer

Translation costs – varies by the translator and type of documents being translated

Original documents/certified copies – varies by case

Legal Fees

The legal fees for a deferred action application will vary by law firm and the complexity of the case. If you decide to work with an immigration lawyer, you should focus on finding the best immigration lawyer for your case. Later in this book I discuss how to find the best lawyer for your case.

Deferred Action Timeline

As of the writing of this guide, no announcements had been made about how long it was expected to take to receive a decision on a deferred action application. The two things that are known at this point are:

1. ***There is no process to expedite your application***. Don't be fooled by promises that someone can help

expedite your application or move your application to the front of the line.

2. The best way to ensure that you get an answer as quickly as possible is to make sure that all of the information on your application is correct and to include supporting documents that leave no doubt that you meet all of the qualifications for deferred action.

Keep in mind that this is a new process. The best thing that you can do is to be patient, check the status of your case online and respond to any USCIS requests for additional information as quickly as possible.

After Submitting Your Deferred Action Application

After you submit your deferred action application, you will be scheduled for a biometrics appointment at your local application support center. The appointment notice will be sent to the address you provided on your application. You should make sure that you follow the instructions on your appointment notice. Keep in mind that the biometrics appointment is an important part of the process. Your application won't be approved if you don't attend your appointment.

You will be able to track the status of your application online at:

ImmigrationVirginia.com/check-deferred-action-application/

If you move after submitting your application, you will need to update your address with USCIS. If you don't, you may miss out on important correspondence from USCIS. For example, if USCIS needs additional information in order to make a decision on your application, they will send you a request for evidence in the mail. If you don't respond to the request for evidence before the listed deadline, your application likely will be denied.

Questions and Answers

How can I expedite the processing of my application?

There is no process to expedite your deferred action application. Anyone who claims to be able to get your application "priority" processing or to be able to use "inside connections" to help get your application moved to the front of the line is not telling you the truth. Don't be fooled by anyone who makes these claims.

What you can do to help avoid any delays is to make sure that all of the information on your application is correct and that the supporting documents you submit with your application are well organized and make it clear that you qualify for deferred action. This will help minimize the chance that you are sent a request to submit additional evidence, which will result in a delay in getting a final decision on your application.

What are the benefits of applying for deferred action?

Many people who are granted deferred action will be able to get employment authorization cards so that they can lawfully work in the United States. In addition, depending on state law, people who receive deferred action may be able to obtain a driver's license or state identification card. However, deferred action does not give you a permanent right to stay in the United States, forgive past immigration violations or give you a way to obtain a green card.

What are the risks of applying for deferred action?

The two greatest risks of applying for deferred action are:

1. Your application is denied and your case is referred to the immigration court for deportation proceedings.

2. The deferred action policy is changed in the future so that you are unable to renew your deferred action status and you are then placed in deportation proceedings.

Although there are some concerns that the information on your application about your family may be used to start deportation proceedings against your family members, at the present time there is no evidence that this will happen. Initial indications from the government are that the information on deferred action applications will not be used to deport family members (provided that there is no fraud on the application or criminal issues in the case).

Can I apply for deferred action if I'm not already in immigration court proceedings?

Yes. You do not need to be in immigration court proceedings to apply for deferred action under the new policy for childhood arrivals.

What happens at the end of my two-year deferred action period?

If the deferred action policy is still in place when your initial deferred action expires in two years, you may be able to apply for an extension of your deferred action status. However, there is no guarantee that an extension will be granted or that the deferred action policy will still be in place in two years.

What happens if I apply for deferred action but don't qualify?

Depending on your situation, your case may be sent to immigration court for deportation proceedings if your deferred action application is denied. Not all denied cases will be sent to immigration court. The government has indicated that applicants who are denied due to criminal convictions or fraudulent applications will have the greatest risk of being deported.

What happens if I lie on my deferred action application?

NEVER LIE TO ANY IMMIGRATION OR GOVERNMENT OFFICIAL OR ON ANY IMMIGRATION FORM. Even "little" misrepresentations can have serious immigration consequences. If you lie on your deferred action application, you will destroy any chance you have of ever becoming a permanent resident or a United States citizen.

Don't be tempted to listen to anyone who tells you to misrepresent anything on your application. It doesn't matter if a family member, friend, immigration consultant, notario or lawyer tells you to lie on your application. You will pay a very serious price for making the misrepresentation.

One of the few things that is known about the deferred action program at this point is that if misrepresentations or fraudulent documents are found as part of your application, your case will be referred to immigration court for deportation proceedings. It won't matter why you submitted the fraudulent application, you will be deported.

When can I get a green card after getting deferred action?

Deferred action does not give you a pathway to becoming a permanent resident or getting a green card. If anyone offers to help you get a green card through the deferred action policy, walk (or run) away quickly.

When can I apply for United States citizenship after getting deferred action?

Deferred action does not give you a pathway to becoming a United States citizen. If anyone offers to help you get citizenship through the deferred action policy, walk (or run) away quickly.

The qualifications said that military veterans qualify. Does this mean I can join the military?

No. The deferred action policy does not authorize the military to allow anyone to enlist who is not currently in a lawful status. As a general rule, if you are not a permanent resident or United States citizen, you cannot enlist in the military. There are limited exceptions to this general rule through the MAVNI program. However, the MAVNI program requires that you be in a lawful immigration status in order to apply.

If I am a military veteran, should I apply for deferred action?

Although being a military veteran may make you eligible for deferred action, you should first check with an immigration lawyer about whether you qualify for United States citizenship. Most people who are military veterans who would qualify for deferred action will also qualify for citizenship through the special citizenship provisions for people who are in the military or who are veterans. If you enlisted in the military by submitting fraudulent documents, you should discuss your case with a qualified immigration lawyer before submitting a citizenship application or a deferred action application.

Is deferred action the same thing as the DREAM Act?

No. The DREAM Act is a proposed law that would need to be passed by Congress and then signed by the President in order to become an actual law. Deferred action is a temporary measure that falls far short of the benefits that would likely be provided by the DREAM Act. For example, the DREAM Act would give young immigrants a way to eventually get green cards and then become United States citizens. Deferred action does not lead to a green card or citizenship.

Is deferred action a new law?

Deferred action is not a law. It is a policy. What does this mean? Simply put, as a policy it can easily be changed. When you go to renew your deferred action in two years, there may be a different policy in place or there may be a law in place that gives you better options. If there is a new policy in place, it could give you better options than the current policy or it could mean that you are placed in deportation proceedings. There is no way to know what will happen over the next two years.

I don't have all of the documents to show that I qualify for deferred action. What options do I have?

You won't be granted deferred action if you can't prove that you qualify. If you are having trouble collecting the documents needed to show that you qualify for deferred action, you should discuss your situation with an immigration lawyer. Your immigration lawyer may be able to help you collect the documents you need.

My conviction was expunged or I was given a diversion program by the judge. Can I apply for deferred action?

In most cases an expunged conviction or a diversion program will still have serious immigration consequences. This is true even if the criminal court judge or a criminal defense lawyer told you that it would be as if "you were never convicted." Immigration law views convictions differently than criminal law. You should always verify any potential immigration consequences of a criminal conviction before you submit any immigration paperwork.

Deferred Action Checklist

Collecting the information and documents that you'll need to prove that you qualify for deferred action is one of the first things that you'll have to do as part of the application process. Although the checklist in this book doesn't cover everything that could come up in preparing your deferred action application, it does provide a good starting point for collecting the information needed for your application.

Supporting Documents

- Documents proving that you came to the United States before you turned 16:
    - Financial records (bank statements, utility bills, rent receipts, tax returns, credit card statements, cancelled checks, etc.)
    - Medical, hospital and immunization records
    - School records
    - Employment records
    - Military records
    - Immigration documents
    - Driver's license
    - Court documents

- Documents proving when you entered the United States
    - Financial records (bank statements, utility bills, rent receipts, tax returns, credit card statements, cancelled checks, etc.)
    - Medical, hospital and immunization records

- School records
- Employment records
- Military records
- Immigration documents
- Driver's license
- Court documents

- Documents proving your birthday
  - Birth certificate
  - Passport

- Documents proving that you have continuously resided in the United States since June 15, 2007:
  - Financial records (bank statements, utility bills, rent receipts, tax returns, credit card statements, cancelled checks, etc.)
  - Medical, hospital and immunization records
  - School records
  - Employment records
  - Military records
  - Immigration documents
  - Driver's license
  - Court documents
  - Children's birth certificates if born in the United States
  - Marriage certificates

- Documents proving that you were physically present in the United States on June 15, 2012:
  - Financial records (bank statements, utility bills, rent receipts, tax returns, credit card statements, cancelled checks, etc.)
  - Medical, hospital and immunization records
  - School records
  - Employment records
  - Military records

  - Immigration documents
  - Driver's license
  - Court documents
  - Children's birth certificates if born in the United States
  - Marriage certificates

- Your high school diploma, school transcripts or proof of your GED

- If you are currently enrolled in school, evidence of your enrollment

- If you are a veteran, your DD-214 or other military records

- Copies of any arrest reports or criminal court documents

- List of any trips outside of the United States since you first arrived, along with a description of why you made the trip and the exact dates of your trip

- If you want to apply for a fee exemption, evidence of your current income and expenses

Additional Items

- Passport photographs. The I-765 form for an employment authorization card typically requires that you submit two passport photographs. It is unclear if additional photographs will be needed for the deferred action application form.

- Biometrics fee of $85.
- Employment authorization card fee of $380

Do I Need An Immigration Lawyer To Help Me Apply for Deferred Action?

There is no requirement to use the services of an immigration lawyer in order to apply for deferred action. But, many people will find the services of an immigration lawyer to be extremely valuable to successfully navigating the deferred action application process. At a minimum, you should consider scheduling a consultation appointment with an immigration lawyer to review your qualifications for deferred action, identify other immigration options that you may have and develop a long term immigration strategy.

What An Immigration Lawyer Can Do For You

You should not hire an immigration lawyer to simply fill out forms for you. Although your immigration lawyer will normally prepare any required forms, this is not the primary role of a lawyer. Your immigration lawyer's main responsibilities are to provide you with sound legal advice, identify legal issues, research and draft legal briefs (if needed for your case), communicate with government officials on your behalf and represent you at all stages of the deferred action process.

An experienced immigration lawyer can:

- ✓ Help minimize the risk of your application being denied by providing you with legal advice on the requirements for deferred action and analyzing your situation and supporting documents

- ✓ Help you to avoid unnecessary delays by keeping your case on track
- ✓ Help you get your application approved without unnecessary delays by ensuring that your application is submitted correctly and with all of the necessary evidence
- ✓ Save you the stress of dealing with USCIS and Immigration and Customs Enforcement (ICE) by communicating with them on your behalf
- ✓ Represent you if the government requests additional information about your case
- ✓ Represent you if your application is denied and you are placed in deportation proceedings
- ✓ Provide legal advice about other immigration options that you may have so that you can make an informed decision about whether to apply for deferred action

In addition, your immigration lawyer will typically help you by:

Verifying that you meet all the requirements before you submit your application.

In some cases, it may not be clear if you meet all of the requirements for deferred action. If you don't qualify, your application will be denied, your filing fee will not be refunded and you may be placed in deportation proceedings. Your immigration lawyer will confirm that you qualify for deferred action and that you have the evidence needed to prove that you qualify. This will help minimize the risk of having your application denied.

Identifying and evaluating all of your possible immigration options.

Your immigration lawyer will help you identify each immigration option that may allow you to achieve your goals. Depending on your situation, you may have more than one option that you could pursue. **You may have better options than deferred action.** Your lawyer will help you determine which option would be the best for you.

In addition, you should keep in mind that deferred action is only a temporary solution and does not provide a path to a green card or forgive any past immigration violations. Your immigration lawyer should be able to help you develop a long term immigration strategy that helps you understand what options you may have in the future to get a green card and eventually become a citizen.

Evaluating whether any criminal convictions will cause problems with your deferred action application.

Many criminal convictions (even misdemeanors) can create serious immigration consequences. If you have **any type** of criminal conviction – even if the conviction was expunged or you were given an alternative sentencing or diversion program – you should let your immigration lawyer know about it. Your lawyer will likely want to review the criminal court records to identify what immigration consequences you may face and if there is any way to minimize or eliminate those consequences.

Many convictions that may not seem to be a "big deal" will disqualify you from getting deferred action. Do not assume that your conviction will not cause you problems. Make sure that someone who is familiar with how immigration law treats convictions reviews your case before you submit your application. If you apply for deferred action but have a disqualifying conviction, you risk being deported.

Assisting you with preparing and filing your deferred action application.

Your immigration lawyer will also assist you with preparing and filing your deferred action application. This will include the correct completion of all of the necessary forms, as well as presenting the necessary supporting evidence in a way that will make it clear to the immigration officer who reviews the package to see that your application should be approved. In addition, your immigration lawyer can research and draft any legal memos that are needed to help make it clear that you qualify for deferred action.

How To Find An Immigration Lawyer For Your Deferred Action Case

Choosing a lawyer to represent you is an important decision. The task of choosing the right immigration lawyer for your deferred action application is complicated by the fact that there are many areas of immigration law. Some lawyers specialize in business or employment immigration issues, while others focus on cases involving litigation, such as immigration court hearings or immigration appeals.

Because the deferred action process for childhood arrivals is a new process, you won't be able to find a lawyer who has years of experience with this particular type of application. However, you should consider asking if your lawyer is familiar with getting immigration court cases administratively closed or terminated through the prosecutorial discretion process which is probably the process that is most similar to the deferred action process for childhood arrivals.

For your deferred action application, you'll want to make sure that you focus your search for a lawyer on those immigration lawyers who accept deferred action cases. It may also be helpful to look for an immigration lawyer who accepts family based immigration cases and immigration court cases so that you know that your lawyer is familiar with the other immigration options that may be available to you.

So, how do you know which lawyer to choose for your deferred action application? The decision of which lawyer to hire should not be made on the basis of advertising alone. *The Yellow Pages* and Craigslist are filled with ads – all of which say basically the same thing. You should not hire based solely on advertising. Instead, you should hire the lawyer that you trust to do the best job on your case. You shouldn't even hire me unless you trust that I can do a good job for you.

You also cannot rely solely on the recommendations of friends and family. The fact that a lawyer did a good job on a friend's DWI case or a relative's divorce does not make him or her the best attorney for your deferred action application. Immigration law is very complex. Just because a lawyer is very skilled in another area of law, that does not mean she will be able to effectively handle the legal matters of your deferred action application. Likewise, just because a lawyer did a good job with your friend's employment-based immigration case, does not mean she will be the best choice for your deferred action application. I cannot stress it enough: Immigration matters are different and difficult, and they require an attorney who is skilled and specifically familiar with immigration law.

I also caution you to avoid relying solely on "directories" of lawyers, especially those claiming to list the "best" or "top" lawyers or those that provide lawyer rankings. The determining factors for where lawyers fall on this list can be very skewed. If the directory doesn't tell you exactly how they select the "best" lawyers or how they rank them, how do you know the rankings reflect what is important to your case? After all, is a lawyer the "best" simply because they paid to be included in the directory? Is it really important how many academic articles a lawyer has published? Are you looking for an academic writer, or an attorney who can successfully prepare and present your deferred action application? You should be careful to avoid blindly relying on the rankings supplied by other people unless you know that those rankings reflect what is important to you.

This does not mean you should altogether ignore directory listings or referral services. Rather, I caution you to be wary of relying on rankings provided by others unless the person doing the ranking can describe how they came up with the rankings and you are confident that the rankings reflect the factors that are important and relevant to you and your case. General directory services can be a useful tool in helping you locate immigration lawyers in your area that you may want to add to your initial list of lawyers to contact. You should also add to your list the lawyers who are recommended to you by friends and family and the lawyers you identify through your own research, including Internet searches.

Which Immigration Lawyer Is Best for You?

How do you find out which lawyer is the best in your area for your deferred action application? I believe there are key questions you should ask. These will help you determine the best lawyer for your case. It will involve some time on your part, but that's a fair price to pay to find the best representation for your case.

The "best" immigration lawyer for you will depend on many things, including your personal preferences. Some important considerations are discussed below. These topics are not in any particular order because what is important to one person may not be important to another. The items discussed below, however, should give you a good starting point in deciding which immigration lawyer is best for you.

Consultation Policy

I've found that many people call my office and ask about my consultation policy before they ask about anything else. If you are choosing an immigration lawyer based on the lawyer's consultation policy, you should make sure that you understand what the lawyer means by "consultation."

For example, some lawyers offer a free phone consultation; others offer free office consultations; and still others charge a fee for consultations. The choice that each lawyer makes is based on many issues.

The most important thing to keep in mind is the purpose of the consultation. Your primary goal in a legal consultation should be to identify whether the lawyer is a good fit for you and your immigration case. You should not expect an immigration lawyer to be able to provide you with detailed legal advice during an initial consultation, especially if the consultation is short or your issues are very unique or detailed. As discussed above, immigration issues are complex. You should not be surprised if a lawyer needs to take a closer look at your case before providing you with specific legal advice.

Think of the consultation as more of a job interview: You are considering whether or not to hire that attorney. Use the consultation to decide if you would feel comfortable working with the lawyer. Also, take note of whether or not the lawyer can describe immigration options to you in a way that you can understand. In many cases, the lawyer may be able to identify the options that should be explored in your case and explain exactly how they would go about identifying the best option for you.

Also keep in mind that a "free" consultation in many cases will be very short and will rarely provide you with any meaningful legal advice. On the other hand, a paid consultation will typically involve a more in depth discussion of your case and will often be a better investment of your time.

Willing To Provide General Information

Is the lawyer willing to provide you with some general information before you hire them? In particular, can they provide you with helpful information to help you decide whether the lawyer is a good fit? You should feel comfortable that the lawyer can and will do a good job for you, is a good personality match for you, and can and does explain things in a way that you can understand.

You should check to see if the lawyer is willing to provide you with some general information so you can get a better feel for whether the lawyer is a good fit for you in all of these important areas. If the lawyer has a website or blog, visit those websites and check them for information that may help you decide if the lawyer is the right lawyer for you. Does the lawyer offer any materials (such as this book) that you can read before you hire the lawyer? Resources that will help you get a better feel for who the lawyer is?

Is the lawyer willing to explain at your initial meeting the basic issues in your case and how she would handle your case? Are they willing to tell you this even before you commit to hiring them? Keep in mind that there is a difference between providing general information and specific legal advice. It is reasonable to ask a lawyer to provide general information or to summarize the steps they would take to identify the best course of action for your case; however, you should not expect to receive legal advice specific to your situation until you have hired the lawyer and the lawyer has had the opportunity to speak with you and review your documents and evidence to learn the details of your case.

Office Location

Depending on your situation, the location of the lawyer's office may also be an important factor in deciding which immigration lawyer is best for you.

I have offices in Reston, Virginia, Fairfax, Virginia and Washington, DC (Farragut Square) where I can meet clients. However, I understand that for many of my clients it can be difficult to take time off from work just to meet with me. I also have clients who live outside of the Northern Virginia area. For these clients I offer to work with them using email, phone/Skype and mail. Provided that my clients are comfortable using email and communicating long distance, this arrangement often allows my clients to greatest flexibility in choosing who they want to work with. If your lawyer's office isn't convenient for you, can they work with you by email, phone/Skype and mail?

Location can also be an issue when choosing between lawyers located in your local geographic area. If you don't have access to a car, does public transportation provide convenient access to the lawyer's office? If you will only be able to take short breaks from work in order to meet with your lawyer, is the lawyer's office located close to your workplace? Is the lawyer such a good match in every other way that you don't mind having a longer drive to visit them for face-to-face meetings and discussions? These are all important questions to ask before choosing a lawyer.

Personality

It is not uncommon for immigration matters to take months or years to resolve. Bearing this in mind, you should consider whether the immigration lawyer is a good personality match for you. After all, you probably don't want to spend months or years working with someone who you simply don't like to be around!

Does the lawyer take the time to explain things in a way that you can understand?

As you already know, immigration law is very complex. Does the lawyer explain the issues important to your case so that you can understand them? The odds are that whatever the issue is, if it is important to your case, you'll want to understand it so that you can make the best decisions and choose the best options for you. Be sure your lawyer can effectively communicate with you.

Lawyer's fee

Most likely, the lawyer's fee will also be a factor in deciding which lawyer is the best one for you. Key items related to the lawyer's fee that you should consider are: value, affordability, and whether the lawyer accepts the form of payment you want to use, such as credit cards.

Although the lawyer's fee may be important consideration for you, you should avoid using the lawyer's fee as your sole basis for hiring a lawyer. In other words, don't go looking for a bargain! You should not simply shop around for the lawyer with the lowest fees – you don't do that when you need another professional such as a doctor or dentist do you? In immigration law you typically get what you pay for. Do you want the best immigration lawyer for you or do you want the cheapest lawyer?

Instead of focusing on the lawyer's fee, you should focus your search on finding the best immigration lawyer for your deferred action application:

- Are you confident in the lawyer's ability to represent you?
- What is the overall value that is being offered?
- What is included with the fee?
- Will you be charged extra for phone calls, online legal research, or postage?

- Will you be charged extra if the government requests additional information in your case?

- Will your lawyer help you develop a long term immigration strategy so that you may eventually be able to get a green card or will they limit their advice to the deferred action application?

You should not assume that you cannot afford to hire an immigration lawyer to assist you with your deferred action application. You may be surprised to learn that hiring an immigration lawyer to assist you can be just as affordable as hiring a non-lawyer immigration consultant.

Language Barrier

Keep in mind that English is the language that will be used to communicate with USCIS. Therefore, you must hire a lawyer who can effectively communicate in English.

At the same time, you should feel comfortable in communicating with your lawyer. If your native language is not English, how important is it to you that your immigration lawyer speaks your native language? If you are not comfortable discussing your case in English and the lawyer doesn't know your native language, would you be comfortable working with a translator? Does the lawyer have someone in their office who can translate, or do you have a friend who would be willing to help? There are no right or wrong answers to these questions. The important thing is that you are comfortable working with your lawyer and that you and your attorney can find a way to effectively and clearly communicate.

Membership in Professional Organizations

Because immigration law is constantly changing, it is important that you hire an immigration lawyer who is able to keep up with the changes. One of the best ways for a lawyer to do this is to join a professional organization such as the American Immigration Lawyers Association (AILA). AILA is a national association of over 11,000 lawyers and law professors who practice and teach immigration law. Among other things, AILA provides continuing legal education and information that helps its members stay up to date with new developments in immigration law. I am a member of AILA and receive daily updates of new developments. These updates help me to ensure that my clients are not surprised by any new developments that may affect them or their cases. If your lawyer is not a member of AILA, you should ask them what steps they take to keep up to date with changes in immigration law.

About Virginia Immigration Lawyer Kimberley Schaefer

When people ask me what I do, I often tell them, "I help future Americans become citizens." After all, American citizenship is the eventual goal of almost all of my clients, and I help them achieve that goal.

I am an immigration lawyer practicing law in Virginia and Washington, DC at Schaefer Immigration. In addition to helping people in Virginia and Washington, DC, I can also help people from throughout the United States with their immigration cases.

I initially became interested in immigration law while completing intensive consular officer training offered by the Department of State at the National Foreign Affairs Training Center in Arlington, Virginia. My interest in immigration law deepened while providing consular services in Lagos, Nigeria. I have an international background and have lived or worked in the United States, Europe, Asia, and Africa.

I also believe that it is important for people to have access to good information about the immigration process when they are trying to decide what the best options are for their immigration case. My website provides helpful information to people before they complete any immigration forms or hire an immigration lawyer:

ImmigrationVirginia.com

In addition, my books such as *Immigration Mistakes You Can't Afford to Make* are also aimed at providing useful information to my clients.

For my clients who are outside of the Northern Virginia and Washington DC area, I work with them using a combination of phone calls/Skype, email and mail. In addition, many of my clients in the Northern Virginia area choose to work with me via phone calls/Skype, email and mail instead of meeting in person at my office. This provides them with greater flexibility on when and how we communicate and allows them to minimize the time they need to take off from work.

For clients who prefer to meet in person, my Reston, Virginia office is conveniently located at the Reston Town Center. I can also meet with clients in Fairfax, Virginia. My DC office is located across the street from the Farragut North Metro station and one block from the Farragut West Metro station, providing my clients with easy access to my office via the Orange, Blue and Red Lines. There is convenient parking in the area and several major bus lines stop within one block of my office.

I am a member of the American Immigration Lawyers Association (AILA), a national association of over 11,000 attorneys and law professors who practice and teach immigration law.

I graduated *magna cum laude* from Georgetown University Law Center and was awarded the Order of the Coif honor in recognition of graduating in the top 10 percent of my law school class. While in law school, I served as the Notes Development Editor of the *American Criminal Law Review*. Prior to attending law school, I served as a communications officer in the United States Marine Corps and worked in both the private and public sectors.

I am licensed to practice law in the District of Columbia. My practice outside the District of Columbia is limited to immigration and nationality law.

About Schaefer Immigration

The main office of Schaefer Immigration is located in Northern Virginia at the Reston Town Center. This office is conveniently located near the Reston Avenue exit on the Dulles Toll Road at:

1818 Library Street, Suite 500
Reston, VA 20190

There are several free public parking garages located at the Reston Town Center.

Additional offices are located in Fairfax, Virginia at:

3915 Old Lee Highway Suite 22-B
Fairfax, VA 22030

And in Washington, DC at:

1000 Connecticut Avenue, NW, Suite 900
Washington, DC 20036

You can contact Schaefer Immigration by phone at:

Phone: (703) 424-2979
Toll Free: (877) 887-9523

If you are interested in setting up a consultation appointment with me, you can contact me at:

AskKimNow.com
or
contact@ImmigrationVirginia.com

NOTES